HEINEMANN Profiles

Paul McCartney

An Unauthorized Biography

Paul Dowswell

Heinemann Library
Chicago, Illinois

Designed by Ian Winton
Originated by Dot Gradations
Edited by Liz Gogerly
Printed and bound in Hong Kong
Produced for Heinemann Library by Discovery Books Limited

05 04 03 02 01
10 9 8 7 6 5 4 3 2 1

Library of Congress Cataloging-in-Publication Data
Dowswell, Paul
      Paul McCartney.
              p. cm. -- (Heinemann profiles)
      Includes bibliographical references (p.), filmography (p.), discography (p.), and index.
      ISBN 1-58810-062-6 (library binding)
      1. McCartney, Paul--Juvenile literature. 2. Rock
      musicians--England--Biography--Juvenile literature. [1. McCartney, Paul. 2. Musicians.
      3. Composers. 4. Rock music.] I. Title. II. Series.

ML3930.M37 D68 2001
782.42166'092--dc21
[B]

00-059746

Acknowledgments
The author and publishers are grateful to the following for permission to reproduce copyright material:
Corbis, pp. 6, 7, 27, 30, 34, 46, 47, 48, 51; Peter Newark's American Pictures, p. 22; Popperfoto, pp. 20, 25, 35; Redferns, pp. 4, 5, 9, 10, 11, 13, 14, 17, 18, 29, 31, 32, 37, 39, 41, 42, 45; Topham Picture Point, pp. 28, 38.

Cover photograph reproduced with permission of E. T. Archive.

Every effort has been made to contact copyright holders of any material reproduced in this book. Any omissions will be rectified in subsequent printings if notice is given to the publisher.

This is an unauthorized biography. The subject has not sponsored or endorsed this book.

Some words are shown in bold, **like this.** You can find out what they mean by looking in the glossary.

CONTENTS

WHO IS PAUL MCCARTNEY?

Paul McCartney began his musical career writing songs with John Lennon. They are regarded as the most **influential** writing partnership in popular music. Their group, the Beatles, is seen as the most successful band of all time. "Yesterday," Paul's best-known **song,** is the most recorded song in history. By the end of the twentieth century, it had been played on U.S. radio more than seven million times.

Even though Paul can play many musical instruments, he does not read music. Nonetheless, his **melodic** bass-guitar playing style has been copied by countless other musicians. He has been the only Beatle to remain in the public eye. After the group split up, John Lennon divided his time between a **solo** career and home life until his murder in 1980. George Harrison and Ringo Starr, the other Beatles, gradually stopped making albums, as their solo work became less popular. Paul remains a high-profile and hard-working rock star. He still plays to huge crowds and sells millions of records.

A MAN OF MANY TALENTS

Paul is a shrewd businessman. His own successful songs, and the **copyright** he owns on stage shows and the songs of other musicians, have made him one of rock's richest performers.

Despite his wealth, Paul has tried to lead as ordinary a life as possible. When he was a Beatle, Paul's face was so well known that he was mobbed whenever he appeared in public. To avoid the attention of fans, he occasionally went out with a false moustache and glasses.

Paul is also a devoted family man. Two of his best loved songs, "Yesterday" and "Let It Be," were inspired by the death of his mother. His long and happy marriage to Linda McCartney was a love story in its own right. All his children went to public schools, and have been carefully guarded from television and newspaper journalists.

Paul returns to a replica of the Cavern Club in Liverpool to publicize his new album "Run Devil Run," in December 1999. The last time Paul played the Cavern was with the Beatles in 1963.

EARLY DAYS

Paul was born at Walton Hospital, Liverpool, on June 18, 1942. He was the first child of Jim and Mary McCartney. At the time, Europe was in the middle of the World War II. Liverpool, which was then Britain's greatest port, had been bombed so badly that two-thirds of the city's homes had been damaged or destroyed.

The McCartneys were not wealthy, but Paul's parents had steady jobs and lots of ambition. During peacetime, Paul's father, Jim, worked as a cotton salesman. However, his salary was never enough to allow his wife to give up her job as a nurse. During the 1940s and 50s, most women left work when they married, and Jim McCartney was embarrassed by the fact that his wife not only worked, but that she earned more money than he did.

LIFE IN THE OUTSKIRTS

When the war ended in 1945, the family moved to a public housing development in Speke on the outskirts of the city. Built to replace some of the 10,000 homes demolished by German bombs, Speke's houses were barely finished. In addition, they all had outside bathrooms and were surrounded by the dirt and chaos of a huge building site. "We were slopping through mud for a year," recalled Paul, looking back on his family's time in Speke. "We were always on the edge of the world . . . there was a feeling you might drop off."

Being on "the edge of the world" meant that it took an hour by bus to get to Liverpool. However, it also meant the McCartneys lived near the countryside. A five-minute bike ride took Paul to thick woods and fields and the wide-open skies and mud-flats of the Mersey **Estuary.** The McCartney family spent many hours bird-watching and hiking, and the experience left Paul with a life-long love of the country and simple pleasures.

Jim McCartney and his famous son in 1964. Paul's father encouraged him to play music from a young age. The two remained close throughout Jim's life.

GREAT EXPECTATIONS

Speke was a rough neighborhood, with its share of bullies and thugs, but Jim and Mary McCartney were determined that their sons would grow up to be respectable citizens. The boys were discouraged from speaking in the local accent by their mother. The whole family would work together to solve the daily newspaper crossword puzzle, and any question Paul or his brother Michael had about the world was resolved by consulting the family's encyclopedias. When Paul won an essay competition at school, he chose as his prize a book about modern artists. It was the start of a life-long interest in paintings and art.

Paul and his family moved to this house in Allerton in 1955.

Paul's parents wanted him to be a doctor. When, at the age of eleven, Paul won a place at the Liverpool Institute, they must have felt he was heading in the right direction. The Institute was the city's best high school. It was on his hour-long journey to the Institute that Paul met George Harrison. George was also studying at the Institute and became one of Paul's best friends. Although Paul was never a great student, the Institute gave him the

GOODGE PLACE

Paul's first car was called a Mini. Success of the Beatles would soon mean that he would trade this humble car for a more expensive vehicle.

confidence to feel there was a life outside working-class Liverpool.

STEPPING UP IN THE WORLD

Paul's feeling of **optimism** was shared by many people throughout Britain. As the country recovered from the war, a generation grew up secure in the knowledge that their world would be different from that of their parents. The British government introduced **social reforms** that made sure that the children in Paul McCartney's generation would be healthier and better educated than ever before.

In 1955, the McCartneys took another step up in the world. The family moved to the middle-class suburb of Allerton. Although they still rented their house from the government, for the first time in their lives they had an indoor bathroom. Money was still scarce, though. Looking back on his childhood, Paul said, "We never had a car. I was the first one in my family to buy a car with my Beatles' earnings."

FAMILY TRAGEDY

The year 1956 brought family tragedy. In October, when Paul was fourteen, Mary McCartney died suddenly. A brave, selfless woman, she had ignored chest pains that had recently troubled her, and did not know that she had developed breast cancer. By the time her condition was discovered, it was too late to save her. "It was very tough to take,'"recalled Paul. "Seeing your father cry for the first time in your life was not easy."

The distraught family was lucky to have a close network of relatives to rally around to help. It was about this time that Paul discovered he had a serious talent for music. His father had given Paul a trumpet, but Paul soon traded it in for a guitar. Paul, who is left-handed, found that if he restrung the guitar upside-down then he could play quite well. The instrument became a major distraction and

Rock and Roll!

Times were changing during the late 1950s. The economy was thriving, and jobs were easy to find. For the first time ever, teenagers had money to spend on clothes and entertainment. They listened to **rock and roll,** and Paul quickly took to this new music, too. He was soon learning the songs he heard on the radio by Elvis Presley, Little Richard, and Chuck Berry.

Paul, wearing a rock and roll hairdo and oozing self-confidence, poses for a school photograph during the late 1950s.

comfort, and Paul took it with him everywhere. At the age of fourteen, Paul wrote his first song, "I Lost My Little Girl." Music gradually became more important than any other subject, even art, which he liked but did not feel he was very good at.

One summer afternoon, shortly after his fifteenth birthday, Paul McCartney put on his sharpest clothes and prepared to wander over to a local church fair. He was hoping to meet a girl there. Instead, he met a fellow teenager named John Lennon. Together, they would change the nature of popular music and become the most successful songwriting partnership of all time.

Quarryman to Moptop

When Paul arrived at the fair, he met a band called the Quarrymen. John Lennon was their lead singer. Because of his aggressive manner, John wasn't easy to get along with, but everything changed when Paul picked up a guitar. He played Eddie Cochran's "Twenty Flight Rock," a song he fondly describes as "the song that got me into the Beatles." The Quarrymen were impressed by his ability to play difficult chords and with "the fiddly bits" in the song. He was in!

Soon after joining the Quarrymen, Paul heard that his friend George Harrison had started to play guitar. George joined the group in early 1958. The band that was to become the Beatles had started to fall into place.

That summer bought another tragedy. John Lennon's mother, Julia, was hit by a car and was killed. Her death affected John very deeply, but the incident brought him and Paul closer. "We were both wounded animals and, just looking at each other, we knew the pain we were feeling," said Paul.

The beatles are born

Like most bands, the Quarrymen played songs written by other songwriters. As the Quarrymen got better, John and Paul started writing songs together. Reminiscing to Guitarist magazine in early 2000, Paul said, "We'd turn up to a **gig** and often there'd be four or five bands on. You'd . . . discover that the other groups were doing your **set.** (That's) the reason John and I began writing our own songs. It was the only way of saving our act."

The original Beatles line-up. Paul is at the piano. John is on the right, and George is second from the right.

After going through various **line–up** and name changes, the group decided to call themselves the Beatles. The name is a play on their style of music, which was known at the time as "beat music." Along with Paul, John, and George there was bass player Stuart Sutcliffe and drummer Pete Best.

A LUCKY BREAK

The Beatles' first big break was a run of **gigs** in the German port of Hamburg in 1960. It was a harsh introduction to the world of show business. The group lived in appalling filth in an apartment behind the screen of a local movie theater—they even washed in the movie theater's bathrooms. They would play long into the night to drunken sailors. Returning to bed at dawn, the Beatles would soon be awakened by booming theater loudspeakers. During their time in Hamburg, Stuart Sutcliffe left, and Paul began playing the bass. They also adopted their famous "moptop" haircuts. In those days, it was daring for men to wear their hair so long. It was an exciting time for Paul, whose encounters with artists and students opened his eyes to a world quite different than the one he'd known in Liverpool.

The Beatles returned to England as experienced professionals who knew exactly how to entertain a crowd. They played regularly at the Cavern Club in Liverpool in 1961, and it was here they first became

In 1960, the Beatles were (from left to right) Pete Best, George Harrison, John Lennon, Paul, and Stuart Sutcliffe.

hugely popular. Fans would line up around the block whenever they played.

POLISHING UP THEIR ACT

The Beatles' popularity attracted the attention of local businessman Brian Epstein. He instinctively knew they could be hugely successful. "I was immediately struck by their music, their beat, and their sense of humor . . . and even afterward when I met them, I was struck again by their personal charm," he told a TV reporter in 1963.

Epstein became their manager, and the first thing he did was polish up their image. He replaced their dated leather stage clothes with daringly cut suits, and then got them a **record contract.** Epstein adored the Beatles with the passion of a true fan. The Beatles, too, were quite aware of his contribution to their success. "If anyone was the fifth Beatle, it was Brian," said Paul.

"This ridiculous style brings out the worst in boys physically. It makes them look like morons." School Headmaster John Weightman, describing the Beatles' haircuts.

READY TO ROCK ...

The group signed with record company EMI. There, they met a Londoner named George Martin, who became their producer. Martin had made a name for himself producing comedy records. He felt an immediate bond with the wisecracking Beatles. But Martin also recognized their musical talent. "He could see beyond what we were offering him," said Paul. Martin felt that drummer Pete Best was weak, so he was replaced by another Liverpudlian named Ringo Starr. The Beatles were set for stardom!

In October of 1962 the Beatles released their first single, "Love Me Do." Paul had begun the song when he was sixteen, and John helped him finish it. It climbed to number seventeen in the British pop charts and stirred enough interest for a follow-up.

... READY TO ROLL

In February 1963, another Lennon–McCartney song, "Please Please Me," topped the British music charts. This was the beginning of an unbroken run of successful singles. The next eleven Lennon-McCartney

"The Fab Four" in 1962. Pete Best's replacement Ringo Starr is on the left. His brilliant drumming was an essential part of the Beatles' unique sound.

In the plush interior of a London hotel, the Beatles and manager Brian Epstein pose for press photographers.

penned singles would also go to number one in Britain. In March of that year, the first Beatles album, also called "Please Please Me," topped the album charts.

That autumn, the Beatles' television appearances caused a sensation in Britain. The newspapers latched on to their popularity, calling the excitement surrounding the band "'Beatlemania." By the end of the year, the Beatles had become a national **phenomenon.** Meanwhile the band had moved to London, which at the time was one of the world's most energetic and exciting cities. Brian Epstein rented a house for them, but Paul found himself in the smallest room at the back. He hated its lack of hominess, but London became his playground. Most nights he went to parties, theaters, and clubs.

"Guitars are out"

Before signing to EMI, the Beatles auditioned for the Decca record company. But executive Dick Rowe dismissed them: "Go back to Liverpool, Mr. Epstein. Groups with guitars are out."

GLOBAL SUCCESS

Soon enough, Beatlemania was strong enough to cross the Atlantic. In January 1964, the Beatles had their first American number-one song with "I Want to Hold Your Hand." It was time for a visit!

The Beatles' arrival at John F. Kennedy Airport in New York that February became a moment that defined an era. The Beatles emerged from a Pan Am 707 to ear-splitting screams that threatened to drown the howling jet engines. Five thousand teenagers, mostly girls, had arrived to greet them.

As the Beatles drove into the city, George Martin recalled, " ... every radio station in New York was playing a Beatles record. You could not turn the dial and not find a Beatles record being played." Before then, Martin had difficulty promoting the Beatles to American EMI executives. "I got increasingly frustrated because [they would say] 'Well, of course. You don't really know about rock 'n' roll in England.'" The American teenagers' reaction to the Beatles showed how wrong those EMI executives had been.

An ecstatic Paul revels in the adoration of the screaming crowd that showed up to greet the Beatles at Kennedy Airport in February 1964.

Police officers keep wary eyes on excitable Beatles fans, who in 1964 mobbed their New York hotel.

CONQUERING HEROES

The Beatles' impact on the United States was astonishing. Here were four guys from working-class Liverpool, playing music invented in America. Until then, rock and roll's greatest performers were American. The Beatles' own idols—Elvis Presley, Chuck Berry, and Little Richard—were all American. Barely out of their teens, John, Paul, George, and Ringo arrived as conquering heroes.

What contributed to their amazing success? For starters, Paul and John had interpreted the music that had influenced them and given it a refreshing twist. "They were doing things nobody was doing," explained Bob Dylan, who was then one of America's most popular folk singers. "Their chords were outrageous, and their harmonies made it all valid. I knew they were pointing to the direction where music had to go."

LOOKING GOOD

Image has always been important to pop success—and the Beatles looked the part. Their daringly tailored suits and outrageously long hair (at least for the time), made them unique. They were also funny, and each Beatle had his own personality. George was dark and mysterious; Ringo was **gawky** and cuddly; John was sharp and witty; and Paul was cute and respectable.

But there may have been another, darker reason the Beatles were so successful. Three months before their arrival in New York, U.S. President John F. Kennedy had been assassinated in Dallas. A glamorous and much admired figure, Kennedy had symbolized the hopes and dreams of the country, and the entire nation was stunned by his death. To the United States press, the Beatles arrived just in time to lift

Beatles on the big screen

In 1964 the Beatles began work on their first movie, *A Hard Day's Night*. The low-budget black and white film was released in July. None of the Beatles had acting experience, so the film was filled with action scenes and humorous one-liners. For Paul, who had become interested in drama, it was exciting to work closely with scriptwriters and actors. In 1965 the Beatles made *Help!* It was filmed in the Bahamas in lavish color. Finally, in 1968 they released *Yellow Submarine*, a feature-length animation.

people's spirits. The Beatles were everywhere, and by April, the top five slots in the U.S. music chart were taken by Beatles' singles.

FAME AND FORTUNE

The Beatles' success with **rock and roll** music opened American ears to other British groups, such as the Rolling Stones and the Kinks. In what music reporters called the "British Invasion," many British performers became international rock stars. Thanks to Paul McCartney and John Lennon, the rock and roll industry is seen by the world as both an American *and* British **phenomenon.**

The Beatles' international success made lots of money for the British economy. In recognition of this success, each of the Beatles was awarded with a **MBE,** or Member of the British Empire medal. The medal is usually given to military heroes and public officials. The award stirred controversy among many British citizens who were offended that pop stars were given such a prestigious award.

Success at a Price

In August of 1965, the Beatles played New York's Shea Stadium to a record-breaking audience of 56,000 people. Eventually, the constant **hysterical** screaming of their fans ruined live performances for the Beatles. Their outrageous popularity also inspired death-threats, and group members even began to fear for their lives.

Looking back on that time, Paul recalled, "As we waited for an armored car to take us to our guarded hotel rooms, I would say to myself, 'I don't want to go through this any longer.'" Their August 1966 concert at Candlestick Park in San Francisco was to be their last ever public performance.

John, Paul, and Ringo check out the sights in New York's Central Park in February 1964. Paul loved the city, but John eventually settled there after the Beatles broke up.

Paul, mugging for the camera. During the mid-1960's, the Beatles' moptops get longer.

But the United States had been very good to the Beatles. Paul fell in love with New York from the moment he arrived. He was thrilled to stand in the places he had seen on TV or in the movies. But Paul was also drawn to New York for personal reasons. In smaller cities in both the United States and Europe, he was constantly surrounded by people who worshiped him, which made even stepping out to the store for a newspaper dangerous. New York was gigantic, and Paul could walk the streets there without being chased by fans. He loved the adoration and wealth that Beatlemania was bringing to him and the other bandmates, but he also longed to lead a normal life.

"Yesterday" and scrambled eggs

Paul wrote one of his most famous songs, "Yesterday," in June of 1965. He woke up with the tune running around his head. "I didn't believe I'd written it. I went around for weeks playing the chords of the song to people, asking them, 'Is this like something [else]?'"

Before Paul wrote the final words, the song was known as "Scrambled Eggs." The opening line was, "Scrambled eggs, oh my baby how I love your legs."

ROCK GOD

For the remainder of the 1960s, Paul and John were rock's ruling partnership. Worshiped by fans as well as critics, they continued to write songs that brought them wealth and popularity.

One of the fads of the 1960s was an interest in Indian religion. This led the Beatles to visit India in 1968.

During the mid-60s, Paul dated actress Jane Asher and lived in her parent's Georgian house in central London. Jane's circle of friends opened Paul's mind to many new ideas. As a boy, Paul had loved art and theater, and being with Jane exposed him to classical music and **avant-garde** theatre, art, and music. This suited Paul, who was anxious to make up for gaps in his education. He was also constantly searching for fresh ideas. At the time, he said, "As far as the Beatles are concerned … it can get dull if we're not trying to expand and move on to other things."

Jane and Paul announced their engagement on Christmas day, 1967, but they split up seven months later.

Meeting Linda

In 1967, Paul met photographer Linda Eastman, an American, at a club in London. Linda's father, Lee, was a well-known show-business lawyer, and she had grown up in a house full of music. Lee was also a great art lover and had collected the work of famous painters. Linda combined her childhood influences of art and music in a career as a photographer. It was in this role that she met Paul. They had a mutual interest in art and a shared affection for the music of their parent's generation.

Like Paul, Linda had also lost her mother at an early age—Mrs. Eastman died in a plane crash when Linda was just eighteen. At their first meeting, Paul was still with Jane Asher, and Linda had her own life in New York. But in 1968, Paul called Linda, who got on a plane to London. They were married in March 1969. Their first child, Mary, was born in August of that year.

Artist Peter Blake's legendary cover for the Sgt. Pepper album showed the Beatles surrounded by photographs of their heroes.

THE SWINGING SIXTIES

Although they had stopped touring, the Beatles were busier than ever. In May 1967, they released "Sgt. Pepper's Lonely Heart's Club Band," an album many regard as the musical high-point of the 1960s. Among their other triumphs were the double album "The Beatles" and the film *Yellow Submarine*.

THE BEGINNING OF THE END

Beatles producer George Martin noted the **rivalry** that lay at the heart of the McCartney-Lennon songwriting partnership. "John sneered at a lot of things, but that was part of the **collaboration** between them. If John did something, Paul would

"Never had it so good ..."

The late-1960s was an extraordinary time to be young. Jobs were even easier to come by than they were during the 1950s, and many social attitudes were changing. Young people really believed they could change the world. They believed that rock music, with Paul and John as their voices, would help to bring about that change.

wish he'd thought of it and go away and try and do something better, and vice versa." But Paul and John would also cooperate. Journalist Hunter Davies, who spent time with the group in 1967 and 1968, wrote: "They'd each give the other bits of songs they'd written. Now and again they'd have written whole songs, but mostly it was half a song, and the other would help finish it."

But all was not well with the band. In August 1967, at the height of the Beatles' popularity, manager Brian Epstein died of an overdose of sleeping pills. He had suffered from depression, and no one knows for sure whether his death was accidental or suicide. Looking back on that time, John recalled, "After Brian died, we collapsed. Paul took over and supposedly led us. But … we went round in circles."

Without Epsteins' peace-keeping talents, the Beatles began to squabble. John and Paul worked more individually than as partners, and Paul and George's relationship began to break down.

DIFFICULT TIMES

In February 1968, the Beatles set up their own company, which they called Apple. Paul explained how he intended it to run.

The Apple Boutique, one arm of the Beatles' business venture, gave away clothes on the day it closed in 1968.

"We want to help people ... we're in a happy position of not needing any more money, so for the first time the bosses aren't in it for profit. If you come to me and say, 'I've had such-and-such a dream,' I'll say to you, 'Go away and do it.'"

Run by friends, the company was a financial disaster. Staff spent money like water, and the office was flooded with unworkable business ideas. The Beatles were losing around tens of thousands of dollars each week, and the group looked for a business manager to rescue them. John, George, and Ringo favored a tough American businessman named Allen Klein, but Paul was eager to use his father-in-law, Lee Eastman. This difference between them would never be resolved and would eventually lead to the ugly end of the Beatles' story.

During this time John had also begun a relationship with artist Yoko Ono. Yoko remained constantly by his side during recording sessions, which irritated Paul and the other Beatles considerably.

"The Long and Winding Road"

Work on their album "Let It Be" was filmed. It proved to be a depressing documentary of the end of the Beatles. Despite this, the album contains two of Paul's best Beatles **ballads,** "The Long and Winding Road," and "Let It Be." Both songs might be considered a reflection of the hurt Paul felt at the slow break-up of the group.

The Beatles' career ended with "Abbey Road," an album that is now regarded as one of their finest. Listening to this last great outpouring of Beatle creativity is exhilarating and sad, and it stands as a great **memorial** to the most creative and influential group of the twentieth century.

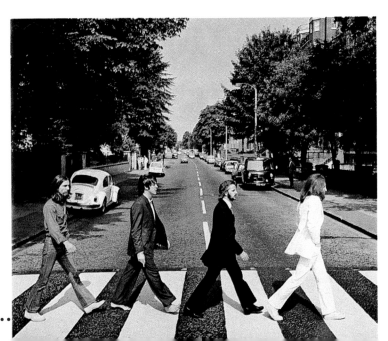

The Beatles walk over a crosswalk outside their recording studio in London. The photo was used on the cover of their final album,"Abbey Road."

OUT OF FAVOR

Although John had told the other Beatles he wanted to leave the group, it was Paul who eventually made the split public. He announced in April 1970 that the Beatles would never work together again.

At the end of the year, on the advice of Lee Eastman, Paul sued the other Beatles to end their business partnership. It was a terribly painful time for Paul, but he was determined to rescue his finances from the influence of Allen Klein, who he was convinced was acting dishonestly.

"I had to take the other Beatles to court. And I got a lot of guilt off that," Paul recalled. That wasn't all he got. Paul won the court case, and the Beatles' financial partnership was dissolved. After the verdict, the other Beatles drove by Paul's London house, and John threw a couple of bricks through his windows.

"THE PARTY'S OVER"

Looking back on the months following the Beatles' split, Paul said, "I found myself in the morning not wanting to get up.... When I did get up I went straight to the whiskey. Luckily, Linda was there. She kept me straight."

"I didn't leave the Beatles—the Beatles have left the Beatles, but no one wants to be the one to say the party's over."
Paul MCartney, 1970.

As he had done in other difficult times of his life, Paul lost himself in his music. In 1970, he released his first **solo** album, which was called "McCartney." On the cover was a photograph of a bowl of cherries. The album contained the catchy single "Maybe I'm Amazed," which is considered by many critics to be Paul's most successful solo song. The album "Ram" followed shortly after.

Divided by squabbles over money, the Beatles were increasingly uncomfortable with each other.

FLYING SOLO

Paul also put a group together with Linda and some other musicians and called it Wings. Although Paul's records sold well, he was out of favor with the critics. They complained that his solo work was shallow. Paul was also seen as "the Beatle who broke up the Beatles." Given their popularity, this was not a happy place to be.

Paul, out on his own, during the early 1970s.

BITTER RIVALRY

Paul's albums may have seemed particularly uninspired when compared with the solo work of John Lennon. At the time, Lennon was hitting new creative peaks with "John Lennon/Plastic Ono Band" and "Imagine." John was even attacking Paul

Paul and John

Paul spoke movingly about his falling out with John Lennon in Barry Miles's biography *Many Years From Now*. "When John did 'How Do You Sleep?' I didn't want to get into a slanging match. I just let him do it, because he was being fed a lot of those lines by Klein and Yoko....Part of it was cowardice: John was a great wit, and I didn't want to go fencing with the rapier champion.... I always find myself wanting to excuse John's behavior, just because I loved him."

in song. In "How Do You Sleep?" John used Liverpudlian street talk to sneer, "The only thing you done was 'Yesterday.'"

During the early 1970s, Paul and John went through several bad years. However, Paul was always eager to patch things up with his old friend, who had moved to the United States. "I would ring him when I went to New York and he would say, 'Yeah, what d'you want?'... It was all very **acrimonious** and bitter," Paul recalled.

John Lennon works on a song with partner Yoko Ono. Yoko increasingly replaced Paul as John's creative partner.

FAMILY AND FRIENDS

The rift between Paul and John was healed by an amazing show of good will by the McCartneys. In 1973, John and Yoko broke up, and John went to live in Los Angeles. During John and Yoko's separation, Yoko visited Paul and Linda in London. The McCartneys were friendly and sympathetic to Yoko, and even agreed to speak to John about getting back together with her. They visited Los Angeles, met with John, and helped to bring John and Yoko back together.

After that, John and Paul were friends again, and when the McCartneys went to New York they would often visit the Lennons. Paul and Linda had a young family at the time, and John and Yoko had just had a son, Sean. The two ex-Beatles would often talk about children.

"People say **domesticity** is the enemy of art … but I made my decision and I feel okay with it. **Ballads** and babies— that's what happened to me."
Paul McCartney, quoted in *Rock–The Rough Guide*.

AT HOME

At the time the McCartneys had three daughters: Heather, from Linda's previous marriage, Mary, and Stella, who had been born in 1971. The McCartney family would be completed by son James, who was born in 1977. Paul's love of children is well-known: "I'd been fortunate to be around a lot of kids. I'm from a big family, so your cousins would dump a baby on you and you'd know how to jiggle it and you became good at it … I've enjoyed being a parent, just never had a problem with it.…"

Paul stands with his family in 1973. Heather hugs her mom, who also carries baby Stella. Daughter Mary stands in front of Paul.

"Band on the Run"

Wearing what passed for high fashion in 1973, Paul's group Wings perform one of their singles in a television studio.

In 1973, Paul McCartney and Wings packed their bags and headed for Lagos, Nigeria, to record a new album. The trip started badly. Paul and Linda were held at gunpoint by armed robbers, and Linda pleaded, "Please don't shoot him! He's a Beatle!"

The new album was called "Band on the Run." It was a critical and commercial triumph and was considered by many people to be the best ever work by a former Beatle. Two singles from the album, "Band on the Run" and "Jet" were huge successes.

Things also began to look up as Paul's relationship with the other ex-Beatles got better. They had eventually realized that Paul had been right to be suspicious of Allen Klein and no longer wanted him to manage their finances, either.

Record sales

In 1975, Wings released their follow-up to "Band on the Run." Unfortunately, "Venus and Mars" was a serious critical and commercial disappointment.

Then, in 1978, Paul released "**Mull** of Kintyre," an album that fans either loved or hated. Other singles, such as "Silly Love Songs" and "Let 'Em In," were also very successful. Paul could still create best-selling records.

"Mull of Kintyre"

Paul has several homes. He bought a farm near the Mull of Kintyre in Scotland during his Beatles days. Its secluded location was a welcome retreat from the spotlight of London and the madness of Beatlemania. "I liked its isolation and I liked the privacy and the end-of-the-world remoteness compared to a city," he explained. Linda loved it, and Scotland, too. '"It was the most beautiful land you have ever seen … so different from all the hotels and limousines and the music business…." she said.

The former Beatle and his wife Linda in the mid-1970s enjoy a quiet moment together.

Downs and Ups

In December, 1980, John Lennon was shot dead in New York by a **deranged** fan. Journalists immediately gathered around Paul's house. Paul commented, "I can't take it in at the moment. John was a great man who'll be remembered for his unique contributions to art, music, and world peace." Then, as he had always done at terrible times in his life, Paul buried himself in work, traveling to a London studio to spend the day recording.

Later that day, Paul was again harassed by journalists eager for a quote. A journalist asked, "How do you feel about John's murder?" Tired and upset, Paul responded, "It's a drag!"

This seemingly uncaring remark was seized upon and widely reported in the press. Paul later explained. "What I meant was ... 'Don't invade my privacy'... When I got home I wept buckets, in the privacy of my own home."

Paul was deeply upset by the death of his childhood friend, but he felt better knowing that he and John had patched up their differences. "I was able to think, at least we parted on good terms. Thank God for that." But cruel remarks in music journals about John's killer shooting the wrong Beatle must have stung.

Global superstar

Wings split up in 1980, but Paul continued to push on as a solo performer. During the early 1980s, he recorded **duets** with two other giants of pop music, Stevie Wonder and Michael Jackson. The resulting songs "Ebony and Ivory" and "The Girl is Mine" may not have suited every fan's taste, but they were huge commercial successes.

Singer and songwriter Stevie Wonder collaborated with Paul on the 1982 pop hit "Ebony and Ivory."

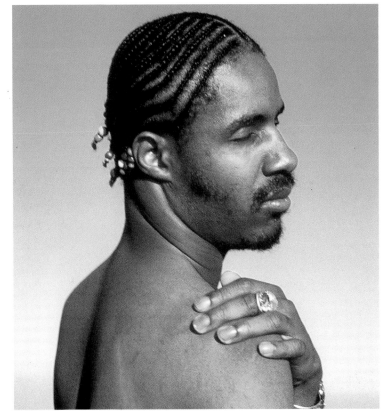

THE SONG IS MINE

While working with Paul, Michael Jackson had asked Paul for business advice. Paul told him to invest in the **copyrights** on songs. During the conversation, Michael joked that he would buy Paul's songs. It turned out that he wasn't joking!

In 1985, the copyright holders of Lennon and McCartney's Beatles' songs put them up for auction. Paul immediately set about trying to buy his songs. But Michael Jackson made a higher bid. This was one of the great disappointments of Paul's life. Jackson still owns these songs, and the two men have not spoken since. Paul learned a valuable lesson from this experience and has since purchased the songs of many other performers and writers.

In a still from Give My Regards to Broad Street, Paul hams it up with old pal and Beatles drummer Ringo Starr.

LIGHTS, CAMERA, ACTION!

In the mid-1980s, Paul made another film. He had been fascinated by the process of filmmaking ever since the Beatles made their own films in the 1960s. But his production, *Give My Regards to Broad Street,* was a failure. The critics hated it and the public stayed away.

Music collecting

Paul's father-in-law Lee Eastman has been a major influence on his business activities. Paul has invested much of his money in music, and with Lee's help has set about acquiring the copyright to an extraordinary collection of music publishing. Paul now owns the music of Buddy Holly and Hoagy Carmichael, among others, and shows such as *A Chorus Line, Annie, Grease*, and *Guys and Dolls.*

Paul and a host of celebrities sing "Feed The World" at London's Live Aid concert in 1985.

But the failure of the film did nothing to dent Paul's worldwide appeal. In 1985, Paul participated in a huge charity concert called Live Aid at London's Wembley Stadium. The concert was broadcast to more than a billion people around the world. Paul closed the show with a solo piano rendition of "Let It Be."

ON TOUR AGAIN

The 1980s ended on another high note. In late 1989, Paul took a new band on world tour. They visited thirteen countries and played to more than three million fans. One of the highlights of the tour was the record-breaking crowd of 184,000 who came to the Maracana Stadium in Rio de Janeiro, Brazil.

AN ARTISTIC SIDE

Paul also has a creative life outside music. Encouraged by Linda and his friend, artist Willem de Kooning, Paul is an enthusiastic oil painter. He has completed many portraits and landscapes. Paul has always had an eye for painting and design, and collects works of art. He painted well at school and helped to design wrapping paper, **publicity** material, and record sleeves during his time with the Beatles. Paul has always felt unsure of this talent. "I felt that only people who had gone to art school were allowed to paint,'" he told

Charity work

Paul, a longtime vegetarian, has supported People for the Ethical Treatment of Animals (PETA). PETA protects the rights of animals through activism, education, and legislation.

biographer Barry Miles. "Then I suddenly thought, this is absolute madness. I'm sure a lot of the great painters didn't go to art college."

Paul said recently "I've been painting a lot for the last ten years. I identify very closely with the caveman who painted on the walls. I'm sure he didn't go to art school, but he had a passion, and he did it."

Paul performs on stage during the early 1990s. Paul's live shows have broken attendance records around the world.

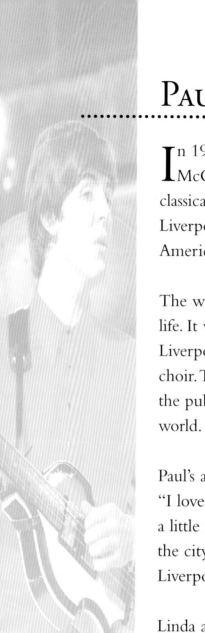

PAUL TODAY

In 1991, the world saw yet another side of Paul McCartney's musical talent. That year, he made his classical music debut with a piece called "The Liverpool Oratorio." The piece was written with American composer Carl Davis.

The work was based on incidents from Paul's own life. It was performed by the ninety-piece Royal Liverpool Philharmonic Orchestra, four soloists, and a choir. The piece was warmly received by critics and the public and has since been performed all over the world.

Paul's affection for his home city remains strong. "I love Liverpool," he said recently, "Every street's got a little memory." Paul also credits his connection to the city with his desire to lead a normal life: "The Liverpool connection's great for that."

Linda also had a yearning to be normal. "She wanted to keep our feet on the ground—for the kids and us both.... We put them through [public] schools instead of Eton and all the posh schools," said Paul.

THE BEATLES ARE BACK!
In 1995, the Beatles' industry (which was still in excellent shape with the re-release of every Beatles'

album on CD) went into overdrive. The remaining band members released *The Beatles Anthology,* three CDs of **demos, out-takes,** and different versions of popular songs. Long available to only the most determined Beatles fan, they were a fascinating insight into the band's creative process. The CDs sold so well that the Beatles were among the top three bestselling artists of 1995.

Paul and his band return to his roots in June 1990. Behind them is the Mersey River in Liverpool. While collecting the "Anthology" material, Paul worked again with the two other surviving Beatles, George and Ringo. They jokingly called themselves the "Threetles," and used a John Lennon demo tape to create two new singles, "Free As a Bird" and "Real Love." The songs were released under the name the Beatles.

PATRON OF THE ARTS

Much of Paul's time in the early to mid–1990s was taken up helping to set up the Liverpool Institute of Performing Arts. The idea for the Institute was inspired by the film *Fame,* which portrayed the lives and ambitions of students at New York's famous School for the Performing Arts. Paul was asked to be the project's chief **patron,** which gave the project much-needed **credibility** and publicity. After six years, Paul had finally raised enough money to build the Institute. Paul was delighted that the building chosen to house the project was his old school, the unused Liverpool Institute.

Paul returns to Buckingham Palace to be knighted by Queen Elizabeth II in 1997.

The new Liverpool Institute was opened in 1996. Today, it offers nearly 200 students courses on working in the entertainment industry.

SIR PAUL

Paul's contribution to popular music was recognized with a knighthood in 1996. Paul attended the ceremony at Buckingham Palace with his children Mary, Stella, and James in March 1997. He told journalists, "This is one of the best days of my life. To come from a **terraced** house in Liverpool to THIS house is quite a journey and I am immensely proud…" He later reflected, "the nice thing about it, (is) when me and Linda are sitting on holiday, watching the sunset. I turn to her and say, 'Hey, you're a lady'. . . although she always was anyway."

Paul and Linda pose for photographers to publicize Linda's brand of vegetarian food.

The 1990s also saw Linda in the public eye. Her own book of vegetarian recipes, *Linda McCartney's Home Cooking,* sold well. She also created her own highly successful line of vegetarian convenience foods.

Paul and Linda had long been known as committed vegetarians. Their compassion for animals is well known. They once bought land in Britain to stop **stag** hunting there. Linda took an especially hard line on the meat trade. "We are doing to animals what Hitler did to humans," she said.

A TERRIBLE BLOW

The decade was to bring yet another tragedy to Paul's life. In 1998, Linda died of breast cancer. She had been suffering from the disease for a number of years.

"I expected us to be 80-year-olds on the porch on our rocking chairs....' said Paul in late 1999. "We fought against [the illness], and did everything we could possibly do. We thought we might have cracked it ... so when she died, it was just a terrible blow for me and the kids."

After a year of grieving, Paul returned to the public eye. He released a critically acclaimed album called "Run Devil Run." Although he had visibly aged, Paul was clear-eyed as he finally spoke fondly of Linda in interviews.

BACK TO HIS ROOTS

As the century ended, Paul returned to his roots in Liverpool to play a **gig** at the Cavern Club. The original Cavern had been torn down in the 1960s, but this was a **reconstruction** of the club in Liverpool's Beatles Museum. Paul's fans were delighted, and his performance sparked renewed interest around the world.

Paul and Linda attend a Paris fashion show in October 1997. On display are daughter Stella's ready-to-wear designs. Linda died the following year.

Paul stands in 1999 before a replica of the Cavern stage. The Cavern was where the Beatles first played nearly 40 years before.

Paul himself has an unusual way of thinking about his own superstar status. "I've always had this thing of him and me; *he* goes on stage, *he's* famous, and then *me*; *I'm* just some kid from Liverpool … occasionally I stop and think, I *am* Paul McCartney … I think it helps keep you sane, actually, if your famous side is a little bit removed from you yourself."

Paul's music has brought pleasure to millions of people. To older people, Paul will forever remind them of their youth and the carefree days of the 1960s. To today's up-and-coming musicians and fans, Paul's songs are an inspiration. Though Paul may still think of himself as just "some kid from Liverpool," he is undoubtedly one of the greatest musicians of the twentieth century.

CHANGING VIEWS OF PAUL McCARTNEY

A COLLECTION OF QUOTES FOR, BY, AND ABOUT PAUL McCARTNEY

"After absorbing every influence from Fred Astaire and Gene Kelly to Little Richard and Elvis Presley, he came forward as Paul McCartney... neither a rocker nor a balladeer, but an extraordinary hybrid from whom sprang 'Yesterday' and 'Lady Madonna.'"

Ray Coleman, *McCartney—Yesterday and Today*

"He's an artist, and artists are moody.... How much pressure has he had, and how many lives has he lived? So he might come on like he's normal, but there's a lot of pressure in there."

Linda McCartney

"People tend to dismiss me as the married ex-Beatle who loves sheep and wrote 'Yesterday'... They think I can write only slushy love songs. My image is more goody-goody than I actually am."

Paul McCartney, *USA Today*, 1989

"That was a songwriting partnership. We were very special. I could feel it was a special kind of thing because it was dead easy to write.... John and I were perfect, really, for each other. I could do stuff he might not be in the mood for; egg him in a certain direction... he could do the same with me."
Paul McCartney, *The Lost Beatles Interviews,* by Geoffrey and Brenda Guillano

During the 1990s, the aging ex-Beatle still showed no sign of slowing down.

List of Films and Records – Singles and Albums

With the Beatles

1962
"Love Me Do"

1963
"Please Please Me"
"From Me To You"
"She Loves You"
"I Want To Hold Your Hand"
Please Please Me (album)
With The Beatles (album)

1964
"Can't Buy Me Love"
"A Hard Day's Night"
"I Feel Fine"
A Hard Day's Night (album)
Beatles For Sale (album)

1965
"Ticket To Ride"
"Help!"
"Yesterday"
"We Can Work It Out"
Help! (album)
Rubber Soul (album)

1966
"Paperback Writer"
"Eleanor Rigby"/"Yellow Submarine"
Revolver (album)

1967
"Strawberry Fields Forever"/"Penny Lane"
"All You Need Is Love"
"Hello Goodbye"
Sgt Pepper's Lonely Hearts Club Band (album)

1968
"Lady Madonna"
"Hey Jude"
The Beatles (album)

1969
"Get Back"
"The Ballad Of John And Yoko"
"Let It Be"
Yellow Submarine (album)
Abbey Road (album)

1970
"The Long And Winding Road"
Let It Be (album)

1994
The Beatles – Live At The BBC (album)

1995
"Free as a Bird"
"Real Love"
The Beatles Anthology 1 (album)

1996
The Beatles Anthology 2 (album)
The Beatles Anthology 3 (album)

With Wings and as a Solo Artist

1970
"Maybe I'm Amazed"
McCartney (album)

1971
"Uncle Albert"/ "Admiral Halsey"
Ram (album)

1972
"Give Ireland Back To The Irish"
Wild Life (album)

1973
"Hi Hi Hi"/ "C Moon"
"Mary Had A Little Lamb"
"My Love"
"Live And Let Die"
Band On The Run (album)
Red Rose Speedway (album)

1974
"Jet"
"Band On The Run"

1975
"Listen to What the Man Said"
Venus and Mars (album)

1976
"Silly Love Songs"
"Let 'Em In"
Wings at the Speed Of Sound (album)
Wings Over America (album)

1977
"**Mull** of Kintyre"

1978
London Town (album)
Wings Greatest (album)

1980
"Coming Up"
McCartney II (album)

1982
"Tug of War"
"Ebony and Ivory" (with Stevie
Wonder)

1983
Pipes of Peace (album)
"The Girl Is Mine" (with Michael
Jackson)
"Say Say Say" (with Michael Jackson)

1984
"No More Lonely Nights"
Give My Regards to Broad Street (album)

1986
Press to Play (album)

1987
All the Best (album)

1989
Flowers in the Dirt (album)

1991
Back in the USSR (album)
Liverpool Oratorio (album)

1993
Off the Ground (album)
Paul Is Live (album)

1997
Flaming Pie (album)

1999
Run Devil Run (album)
Working Classical (album)

FILMS

WITH THE BEATLES
1964
A Hard Day's Night

1965
Help!

1967
Magical Mystery Tour

1968
Yellow Submarine

1970
Let It Be

SOLO
1981
Paul McCartney and Wings—Rockshow

1984
Give My Regards to Broad Street

1991
Paul McCartney— The Liverpool Oratorio

1997
Paul McCartney—Standing Stone

GLOSSARY

acrimonious causing bad feeling

anthology collection of an artist's work

avant-garde art that is considered daring and experimental

ballad slow, gentle song

collaboration partnership on a project between two or more people

composition musical work

copyright legal ownership of a song or written work

credibility respect and trust in the honesty of an artist's work

demo rough preliminary recording not intended to be sold to the public

deranged mentally unstable

duet song sung by two people

estuary part of the ocean at the lower end of a river

gawky clumsy and awkward

gig slang term for a musical performance, usually by a pop musician

hysterical frenzied emotional state, especially including uncontrollable crying, screaming, or laughing

influential So original that people want to copy what you are doing

line-up members of a group

melodic musical term meaning pleasantly tuneful

memorial statue or other object that remembers a person who has died

mull Scottish word that means "island"

optimism state of mind in which one expects things to improve or to turn out for the best

out-take recording that is not released to the public

patron powerful person who supports a particular individual or cause

phenomenon unusual and remarkable occurrence

publicity something that brings a matter to the attention of the public, such as a news story

reconstruction building erected or renovated to resemble one that was built long ago

record contract agreement between a group or individual and a record company in which the company sells recordings produced by that group or individual

rivalry competition between people, sometimes aggressive or driven by ill-feeling

rock and roll style of music developed during the 1950s that features drums, guitars, and a strong beat

royalty payment made to artists whenever their work is sold or performed

set group of songs that a musician performs in public

social reform policies approved by the government and intended to make life better for poor people or minorities

solo performing as an individual artist, rather than as a member of a group

MORE BOOKS TO READ

Venezia, Mike. *The Beatles.* Danbury, Conn.: Children's Press, 1997.

Woog, Adam. *The Beatles.* San Diego: Lucent Books, 1997.

INDEX